GAMES
TO PLAY
WITH THE
VERY YOUNG

by Polly Berrien Berends

Illustrated by
Denman Hampson

Random House

Contents

eeny, meeny, miney, moe.

How to Choose IT

In almost every game, somebody has to be IT. In some games everyone wants to be IT, and in others nobody does. Here are three ways to choose IT fairly and without argument.

Eeny Meeny Miney Moe

Players stand in a circle. One player recites the verse below and points to each of the players (including himself) in turn as he says each word. The player to whom he says the last "Moe" is IT.

> *Eeny, meeny, miney, moe.*
> *Catch a tiger by the toe.*
> *If he hollers, let him go.*
> *Eeny, meeny, miney, MOE!*

3

One Potato, Two Potato

Players stand in a circle, with one person in the center. Everyone makes both hands into fists and holds them out in front, thumb side up. The player in the center turns around the circle, tapping each of the fists with one of his own. (He taps his own in turn.) While he taps the fists, he recites the verse below:

One potato, two potato, three potato, four,
Five potato, six potato, seven potato, more.

He should touch a different fist each time he says a number or the word "more." Every time he says "more," the player whose fist he is touching must hide the fist behind his back. The last player to have both fists eliminated is IT.

Straw Draw

One player picks a straw for each member of the group, including himself. (One straw must be longer than all the rest.) The player holds them in his hand so that just one end of each straw is showing. Then each of the other players draws one straw. The person holding the straws keeps the one which remains after everyone else has chosen. Whoever has the longest straw is IT. (Small sticks, blades of grass or slips of paper may be used if straws are not available.)

Active Games

Statues

Where: Outdoors
How many players: 3 or more
Equipment: None

    One of the players is chosen to be statue maker. He takes each player by the hands, spins him around, and lets go. The player must "freeze" into a statue in whatever position he lands. When all the players have been turned into statues, the statue maker tries to make them laugh or move. The first person to move (either from laughter or fatigue) becomes the next statue maker. *No tickling allowed!*

Cherry Drop

Where: Outdoors or indoors
How many players: 3 to 10
Equipment: A blindfold

One player is chosen to be the cherry tree. He is then blind-folded and must stand with his arms and fingers outspread. Each of the other players (they are all called "cherries") holds onto one finger of the blindfolded player. The cherry tree then asks, "Are you ready?" When the players answer that they are, the cherry tree counts to ten as quickly as possible and all the players run from the tree. As soon as he reaches ten, the cherry tree yells, "Cherry drop!" All the players must stop running and stand still. Remaining blindfolded, the cherry tree tries to find each of the "cherries" that has "dropped from the tree." The last player to be found wins and becomes the next cherry tree.

Redlight, Greenlight

Where: Outdoors
How many players: 3 or more
Equipment: None

One player is chosen to be IT. The other players stand in line about 20 or 30 feet away from him. The player who is IT turns his back to the others and says, "Greenlight, one, two, three, four, five, six, seven, eight, nine, ten, redlight!" As soon as he says "greenlight," the other players begin running toward him. But when he says "redlight," he will turn around and the other players must stop. Anyone he sees moving after he says "redlight" must go back to the starting line.

This is a game where players are sometimes allowed to "cheat." The leader often turns his back and waits a moment before saying "greenlight." The other players may then try to move ahead without waiting for him to begin. But the IT player may suddenly turn around without counting to ten and saying "redlight." Anyone he sees moving must return to the starting line. The first player to tap IT on the shoulder wins and becomes the next IT.

Captain, May I (Giant Step)

Where: Outdoors
How many players: 3 or more
Equipment: None

One player is chosen to be captain. All the other players stand in line, at least twenty feet away, facing him. The captain tells each player in turn what kind and number of steps to take. Before actually taking any steps, the player must say, "May I?" The captain will then say, "Yes, you may," or "No, you may not." If he says no, he will then vary his instructions and, once more, the player must ask, "May I?" Once the captain has said, "Yes, you may," the player is allowed to move ahead in the manner that the captain has permitted. But if a player takes any steps without first saying, "May I?" he must go all the way back to the starting line. The first player to touch the captain wins and becomes captain for the next game.

This is another game in which players are permitted to "cheat." While the captain is talking to one player, the others may try to sneak a little bit closer. But if the captain catches them *in the act* (not after they have stopped) he will send them back to the starting line.

The kinds of steps used in this game are as follows:

1. Giant step: The biggest possible walking step a player can take.

2. Baby step: The smallest possible step. The player must put the heel of one foot against the toe of the other.

3. Banana-split step: Keeping the right foot in place, the player slides his left foot forward as far as possible. He then brings the right foot up beside the left.

4. Umbrella step: The player puts one hand on his hip and the other on his head. Then he jumps up and spins around once, at the same time trying to move forward. (The player will not always land directly facing the captain. This can make future steps even more fun.)

5. Scissors step: Player jumps twice, landing once with his feet spread apart and once with his feet together.

6. Jump step: Player jumps forward, keeping both feet together.

7. Hop step: Player hops forward on one foot.

8. Leap step: Player stands on one foot and lands forward onto the other.

9. Backward step: Any of the above done backward toward the captain.

Jellyroll

Where: Pavement
How many players: 2 or more
Equipment: 1 piece of chalk

Using a piece of chalk, draw a "jellyroll" on the sidewalk and mark it off in sections of various sizes. (See the example below.) The game can be made harder or easier depending on the length of the jellyroll and the size of the sections. Each section or square should be big enough for one foot to fit inside without touching any lines. In turn, the players try to hop on one foot from one section to the next until they reach the center of the jellyroll ("home"). Players must step in each section without touching any lines. If a player steps on a line, he is out until his turn comes again. When a player succeeds in getting to "home," he may rest both feet (still without touching any lines) before attempting to hop back out of the jellyroll again. He may choose to switch feet before hopping out again.

When a player manages to get to the center and back again without any mistakes, he may mark his initials in any square he chooses. From then on, he may rest both feet in that square, but the other players must hop over it. The game is finished when all the sections of the jellyroll are filled with initials. The player who has the most squares with his initials in them is the winner.

Seven Up

Where: Outdoors or in the basement
How many players: 1 or more
Equipment: 1 rubber ball or tennis ball

This game may be played in competition or alone. A player performs, in order, each of the steps listed below. There are seven stunts, each one harder than the one before. When the game is played in competition, a player may continue until he misses. As soon as he misses, the next player takes his turn. When it is the first player's turn again, he must start with the stunt which he missed before. The first person to do all the stunts is the winner. After the players become expert, they may want to vary the rules so that a player must start all the way back at the beginning after each miss.

The stunts should be done in the following order:

1. Toss the ball against a wall and catch it. Do this seven times and then say, "Seven up!"

2. Bounce the ball on the ground and catch it. Do this six times and then say, "Six up!"

3. Bounce the ball on the ground so that it hits against the wall before you catch it. Do this five times and then say, "Five up!"

4. Toss the ball against the wall and let it bounce on the ground once before catching it. Do this four times and then say, "Four up!"

5. Put one arm straight out with your hand against the wall. Toss the ball over the arm that is touching the wall and catch it with your free hand. The ball must not touch the wall and the wall hand must not leave the wall. Do this three times and say, "Three up!"

6. Toss the ball against the wall and allow it to bounce just once. Turn around once before catching it. Do this two times and say, "Two up!"

7. Toss the ball against the wall and let it bounce on the ground two times before catching it. Then say, "One up!"

There are many variations to this game. The players may omit some steps to make the game easier or add their own variations to make it more difficult.

Hide-and-Seek

Where: Outdoors or, *with permission*, indoors
How many players: 3 or more
Equipment: None

The players agree on a place to be called "home" (such as a tree or a lamppost). The player who is IT hides his eyes against home and calls, "On your mark, get set, go!" He then begins counting loudly to fifty or one hundred (the number is agreed on in advance). Meanwhile, the other players run and hide. If the player who is IT is too young to count, the players may agree on a song for him to sing instead. When he finishes counting or singing, he calls loudly, "Ready or not, here I come," and all the players must stop wherever they are.

Then IT begins to look for the other players. When he sees a player, he runs back to home and, while touching it, calls, "Tap tap on Jimmy [or whatever the player's name is] behind the garage [or wherever the player is hiding]." IT must be touching home and he must name the player and his hiding place. If he is correct, then Jimmy must come home, stay home, and be IT in the next game. If Jimmy knows in advance that he has been seen, he may try to beat IT home. Should he succeed in getting there first, he may call, "Home free!" This means Jimmy is safe and doesn't have to be IT in the next game.

Whenever IT is away from home, the other players may choose to leave their hiding places and race to touch home, calling, "Home free!" But if IT beats the hiders to the home base, he can call "Tap tap" on them.

The first person who is successfully caught will be IT in the next game *unless he is freed*. The last person home, and *only* the last person, may "free" the other players. This is possible if he gets there before being "tapped" by IT, and if he calls, "Home free all!" When this happens, the IT player will again be IT in the next game.

In cases where the game has gone on for a long while and there are still one or two players who cannot be found, IT may choose to end the game by calling, "Ally, ally, all in free!" The remaining players will then triumphantly return home. (This is also a good way to end the game if somebody has to go home for supper.)

Tag Games

Where: Outdoors
How many players: 3 or more
Equipment: None

In most tag games, it is helpful to pick one spot that is called "home." No player may be tagged when he is touching home. Sometimes the players will also want to agree on boundaries (especially in Hot Spot Tag).

Touch Tag

The player who is IT tries to tag the other players, who run away from him. When IT finally succeeds in touching someone, that person becomes IT.

Shadow Tag

Instead of tagging the players, IT tries to jump on somebody's shadow. If he succeeds, the player whose shadow he jumps on becomes IT. (Choose an area with lots of sun and few trees.)

Hot Spot Tag

In this game, when a player is tagged and becomes IT, he must put one hand on the spot that was touched. Then he must try to catch one of the others while holding onto his "tag spot." The previous IT is free to run with the others.

Before beginning this game, the players should agree on boundaries. This makes the game fairer, since IT cannot run as freely as the others. If the play area is limited, IT has a better chance of tagging another player. Any player who runs "out of bounds" is automatically IT.

Stoop Tag

This game is played like touch tag, but instead of having a home base the players are safe whenever they are stooping.

15

Quiet Games
School

Where: Stairs (indoors or outdoors)
How many players: 3 or more
Equipment: Pebble, button, or other small object

One player is chosen to be the teacher. He stands facing the rest of the group, or "class," which sits on the bottom step of the staircase. This step is "first grade."

Holding his hands behind his back, the teacher hides the pebble in one of his hands. He then makes a fist of both hands and holds them out toward the group. One player is asked to guess which hand has the pebble. If he guesses correctly he may move to "second grade," the second step. This procedure is repeated in turn with each member of the "class." Whenever a player guesses correctly, he moves to the next step. When he misses he must move down one step (back a grade) or, if he is only on the first step, he stays where he is. The first player to reach the top step wins ("graduates") and becomes the next teacher.

Poor Kitty

Where: Indoors or outdoors
How many players: 3 or more
Equipment: None

One player is chosen to be Kitty. The other players then sit in a circle with Kitty in the center. Kitty crawls around the circle. Every time Kitty stops in front of someone, that player must stroke Kitty's hair, look him or her in the face, and say, "Poor Kitty!" three times without smiling. Kitty, acting like a kitten, tries to make the player laugh or smile. If Kitty fails to do so, he or she moves on to the next player. The first person to laugh becomes the next kitty. *Tickling is not allowed!*

Simon Says

Where: Anywhere
How many players: 3 or more (the more the better)
Equipment: None

All players sit or stand facing a leader. The leader, called "Simon," then calls out simple commands, such as to touch toes, clap hands, sit down, or stand up. Each time he gives a command to the group, he does the same thing himself. Most of the time the command will begin with the words "Simon says...," and the group should then follow the leader's instructions. But when the leader does *not* begin with "Simon says," the group should not follow the new command. They should continue doing the previous one. The players should follow the leader only when the command begins with "Simon says." Anyone who follows a command that does not begin with these words is out. The last person to be eliminated wins and becomes the new Simon.

For the leader, the trick is to get the group moving rapidly to "Simon says" commands and then switch suddenly to a simple "Do this," or "Sit down." A typical sequence might be as follows:

"Simon says, 'Stand up.'" (Leader and group both stand.)

"Simon says, 'Nod your head.'" (Leader and group both nod.)

"Simon says, 'Touch your toes.'" (Leader and group both touch toes.)

"Simon says, 'Touch your shoulders.'" (Leader and group both touch shoulders.)

"Touch your toes." (Leader touches toes, but group should continue touching shoulders.)

Clap a Song

Where: Anywhere
How many players: 2 or more
Equipment: None

One player claps out the rhythm of a familiar song, such as "Three Blind Mice" or "The Farmer in the Dell." The other players try to guess what song he is clapping. The first player to guess the song wins. The winner may then "clap a song" for the others.

Hot and Cold

Where: Indoors or outdoors
How many players: 3 or more
Equipment: None

One player is sent out of the room. While he is out, the other players think of an object for him to guess. Then they call back the absent player. He must move about the room trying to find the object. When he is far away from it, the other players say "cold," but as he gets nearer and nearer to it they say "warm," and "warmer." When he is very near, they say "hot." The player has three chances to guess what the object is. He may guess at any time, but he is wise to wait until he hears that he is "hot," and very close to the object.

This same game can be played by replacing the "hot and cold" signals with clapping. When the player is far from the chosen object, the clapping will be very quiet. It may even stop altogether. But as the player gets "warmer," the clapping becomes louder. When it is *very* loud, the player knows he must be right beside the object.

Everyone takes a turn at guessing until all have had a chance to play.

Travel Games

Alphabet Game

Where: Car, bus, or train
How many players: 2 or more
Equipment: None

Each player tries to find, *in order*, all the letters of the alphabet on the signs along the road. He must call out the word in which each letter is found (for instance, "A and B in *BOATS!*" or "C in FRENCH RESTAURANT!"). If he cannot read, he may describe and point to the sign. ("B in that yellow sign over there!") More than one letter may be taken from one sign. For example, QUAKER STATE signs are wonderful for Q, R, S, T, and U. Whoever sees a sign first gets the first choice of letters on it. The other players are then free to choose any letters he hasn't used. Only one use can be made of each letter; two players cannot select the same one.

Letters may be taken from any sign *outside* the vehicle in which the players are riding. This includes license plates from other cars, traffic signs, billboards, store windows, etc. The first person to reach Z (this and X are the two hardest letters to find) is the winner.

To simplify this game, it is helpful to make each letter or group of letters a "round," giving one point to the winner of each round. For example, the leader (an older child or an adult) may call out "A!" or "A, B, C!" The first player to find the letter or letters wins the round and receives one point. At the end of the game, the player with the most points is the winner.

I'm Going on a Trip

Where: Anywhere

How many players: 2 or more

Equipment: None

The players take turns saying, "I'm going on a trip and I'm going to take a—," naming one thing that they will take on their trip. The trick is that each player must repeat, *in order*, all the things that the people before him have said. After he has done so, he may add something new. For example, a game might begin as follows:

First player: "I'm going on a trip and I'm going to take a suitcase."

Second player: "I'm going on a trip and I'm going to take a suitcase and a kangaroo."

Third player: "I'm going on a trip and I'm going to take a suitcase and a kangaroo and pink pajamas."

A player is OUT when he misses, either by leaving something out or by mixing up the order. The last person OUT is the winner. He may begin the next game.

Quad-ru-ped

Where: Car, bus, or train
How many players: 2 or more
Equipment: None

The object of this game is to see who can count the greatest number of quadrupeds (four-legged animals). The person or team sitting on the right side may count all the four-legged animals on the right-hand side of the road, while the person or team on the left may count those on the left-hand side of the road. Animals found *on* the road count according to the side of the road on which they are found. Each four-legged animal is worth one point, but if the vehicle passes a graveyard, this wipes out all the points for the players on whose side the graveyard is located. Before beginning the game, the players may agree on one animal which will be worth ten points. The "ten pointer" should be something that is not seen often—a white horse, for example.

Bi-ped

Where: Car, bus, or train
How many players: 2 or more
Equipment: None

This game is played in the same way as Quad-ru-ped, except that it is restricted to two-legged animals, not including people. To avoid complications, birds in flight may not be counted.

23

Pretend and Seek

Where: Anywhere (especially on car trips)
How many players: 2 or more
Equipment: None

This is an excellent game to play in the car. The IT player picks out an imaginary hiding place somewhere in the car, such as the gas tank, his own wallet, or the glove compartment. The other players then try to guess where he is hiding. They may ask only questions which can be answered by a yes or no. In the beginning the questions should be general. "Are you hiding in the front of the car?" "Are you somewhere in the dashboard?" Then, when the general area is known, the players may begin to ask more specific questions: "Are you in the ashtray?" The first person to guess the exact spot wins and becomes the next person to "hide."

One variation which makes the game more difficult is to allow the players only a certain number of guesses. The group as a whole may be allowed only 20 general questions. After the 20 have been used up, each player might be given only 3 chances to pick out the exact hiding place. This makes the game more difficult, but it also shortens each round.

For another variation, places *outside* the car might be chosen, but they should be places that all the players know well. If the player chooses to hide outside the car, he must begin by telling what general area he has picked. For example, he might say, "I am hiding somewhere in our house." The others then proceed to ask questions in the usual manner until someone guesses the hiding place. The winner chooses the hiding place for the next game.